AF437375

www.stirredcreations.com

ABCs
IN SPACE
ILLUSTRATED BY
DAISY SUD

A
IS FOR
ASTEROID

B
IS FOR BLACK
HOLE

C IS FOR COSMOS

D
IS FOR DARK MATTER

E IS FOR EARTH

F
IS FOR FALLING
STAR

G
IS FOR GALAXY

H
IS FOR HUBBLE
SPACE TELESCOPE

I
IS FOR
INTERPLANETARY

J
IS FOR JUPITER

K
IS FOR KUIPER
BELT

L
IS FOR LUNAR
ROVER

M
IS FOR MOON

N
IS FOR NEPTUNE

IS FOR ORBIT

P

IS FOR PLANETS

IS FOR QUASAR

R
IS FOR ROCKET

S
IS FOR SATURN

IS FOR
TELESCOPE

U
IS FOR URANUS

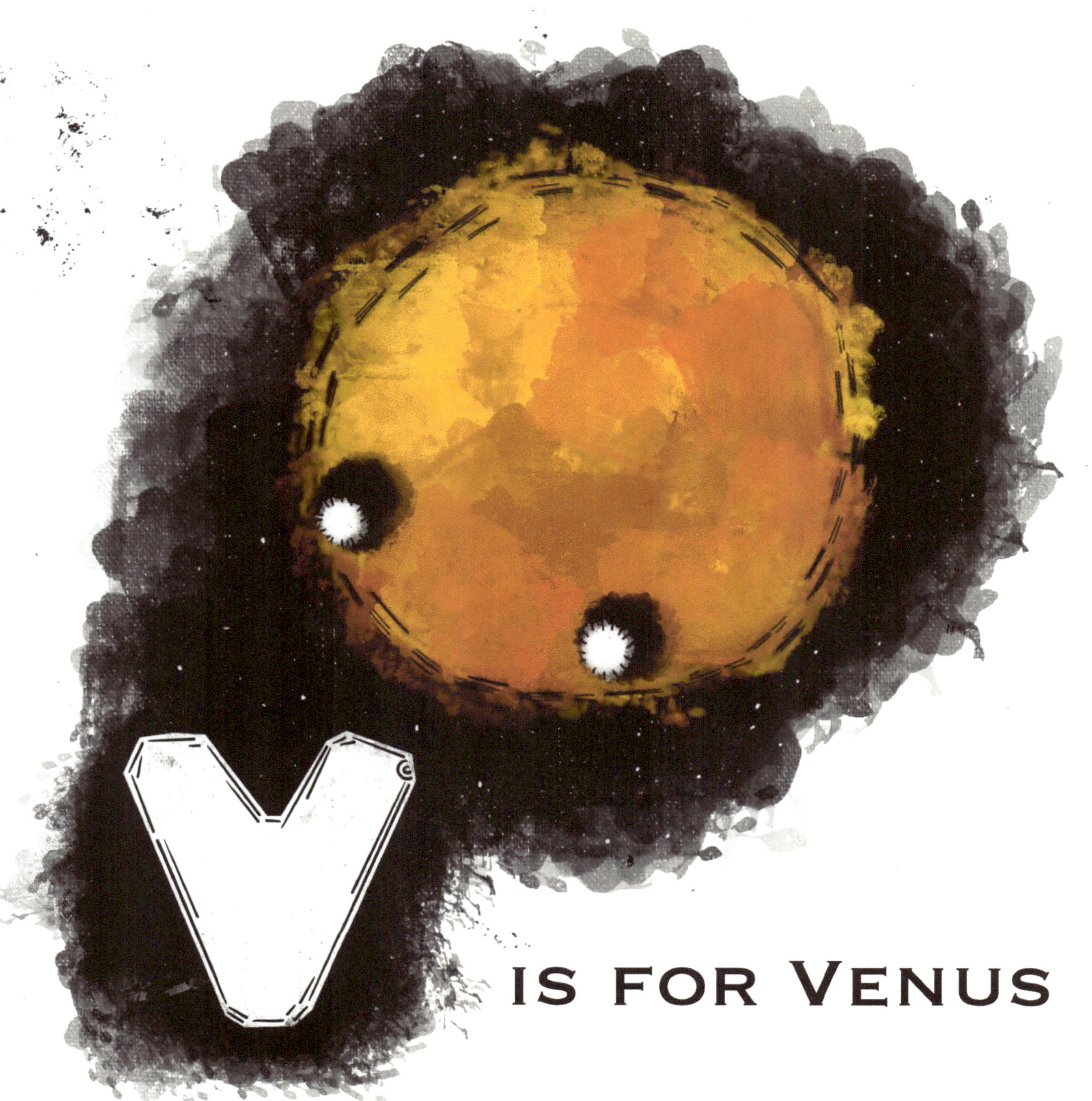

V
IS FOR VENUS

W
IS FOR WHITE
DWARF

X
IS FOR
X-RAYS

IS FOR YELLOW
DWARF

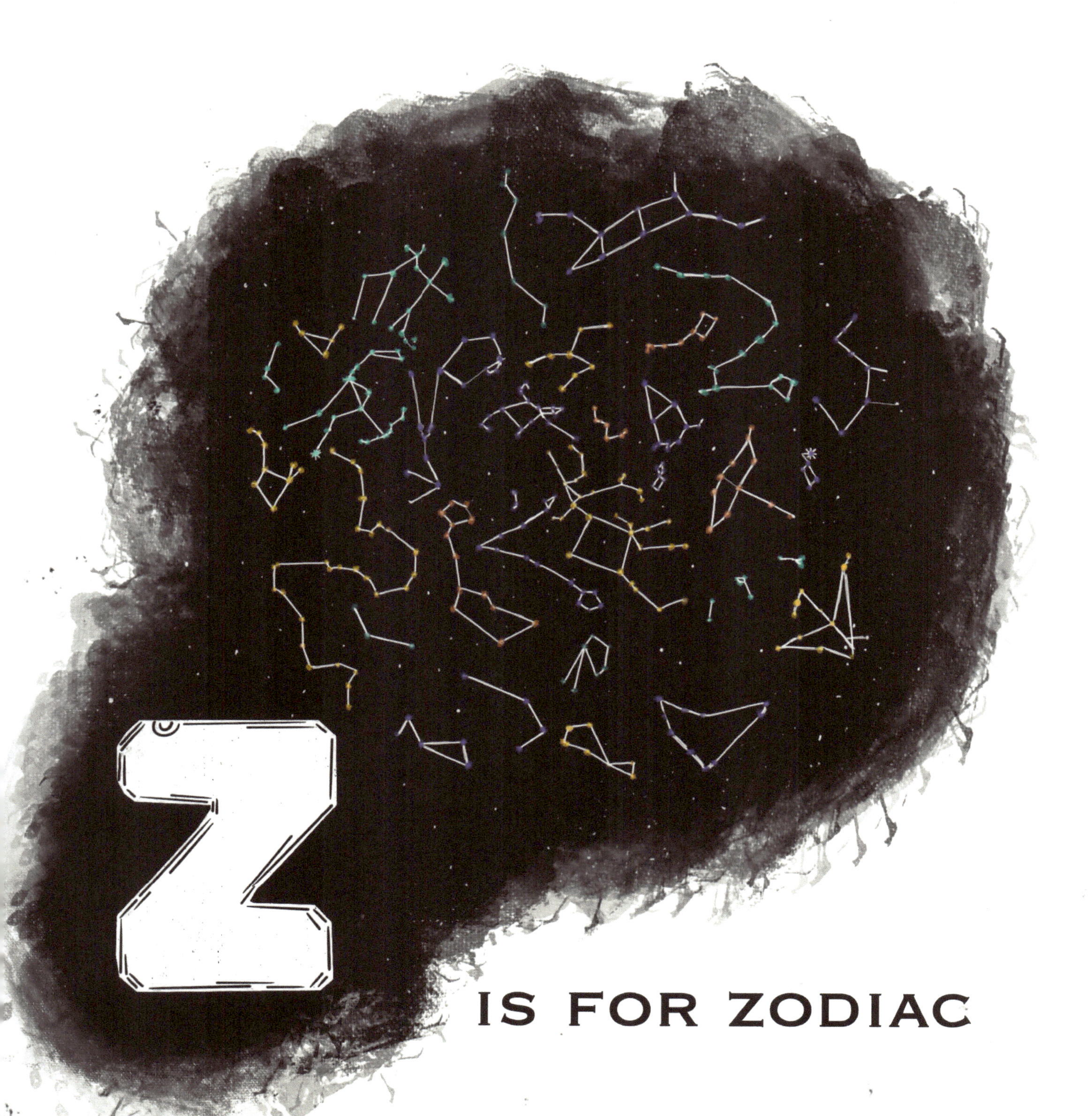

Z

IS FOR ZODIAC